Wanna Know a Secret?

****

A Guide for Youth That Will Teach the Secrets of Life

Cassie Lee Newell

PublishAmerica
Baltimore

© 2008 by Cassie Lee Newell.
All rights reserved. No part of this book may be reproduced, stored in a retrieval system or transmitted in any form or by any means without the prior written permission of the publishers, except by a reviewer who may quote brief passages in a review to be printed in a newspaper, magazine or journal.

First printing

PublishAmerica has allowed this work to remain exactly as the author intended, verbatim, without editorial input.

ISBN: 1-4241-8844-X
PUBLISHED BY PUBLISHAMERICA, LLLP
www.publishamerica.com
Baltimore

Printed in the United States of America

Biography

My name is Cassie Lee Newell. I am twenty nine years old, and a mother of two. I have a wonderful daughter named Phoenix, and a just as wonderful son named Rayne. They are what keeps me going when I feel like giving up. I have grown up all over Alberta and Saskatchewan and have decided to permanently reside in a small city in Alberta called Medicine Hat. My family is all here which makes it home to me for sure. I have been through a lot of ups and downs in my life, some really good, and some really bad, and I feel the need to pass on to others what I have learned along the way. I truly believe that all my life I was learning the secrets that would help me become who I am today. The younger generation of our world deserve to know as well so that they too can become great people in our society. It gives me great pleasure to be able to pass on this knowledge to others, with hopes that they may be able to overcome life's struggles just a little bit easier. I was not always so focused and sure of myself as I am today, but if my life was to be as difficult as it has been in order for me to learn and pass on these secrets then I am grateful for all that is was. I am a better person today because of my struggles and I wish for anyone who reads this guide that they too will be able to say the same. I wish for myself true happiness and joy for all my days to come, and I wish this for everyone else in this world as well...

* Be the best that you can be, and all will work out for the best, you'll see... *

* Cassie Lee *

Be Yourself

    Whoever you are, and whoever you will be is perfect. Never try to change anything about whom you are or how you look. Exactly how you are is exactly how you are supposed to be. A lot of us try to imagine how different our lives could be if we were just a little bit more like someone else. Maybe a girl or a guy from a magazine, or the friend that has it all. Growing up can be hard enough without the extra stress of wanting to be different then what we really are. Why waste time changing when you can spend more time just being you? Think of all the time you would have to just have fun and try new things if you weren't trying to be a new person. Enjoy yourself.

    When I was growing up I constantly compared myself to others. Either girls in my class, or celebrities, and even girls in my own family. I would stare at them and just be completely envious of every feature they had that I didn't or even just their life in general. I would cut out magazine pictures of girls and hang them on my walls hoping that magically during the night I would become more like them and my dreams would finally come true. No such luck, as always I was just who I was when I went to sleep. I was me. Looking back I see how much pain I caused myself and I wish I could have just been happy with who I was. Being older now I look back with sadness because I was perfectly fine and if I could do it all over again I would have spent more time playing or exploring who I really was then trying to change myself. You should too.

Be true to yourself and you will enjoy true happiness. Only you can decide what is right for you. No matter how hard people try to tell you what is right for you they will never truly know for sure. Growing up is about learning whom you are, and what it is you want for you. There are some people who seem to really not know what it is they are doing or where they are going. It may seem that they don't but only they will really ever know. Just like you. Putting pressure on yourself to become what you believe others want you to be will only waste your time. Even if you can't express this to certain people you can always remember that it is true. Deep down you know who you will become one day and when that time comes they will see for themselves.

Besides the fact that trying to be someone you are not will take all of your time, it is also impossible. Completely and truly impossible. Don't forget this okay, you will always be who you are, and no amount of dreaming can change this. We are all precious in our own way, and you are too. Embrace the uniqueness of yourself and you will begin to discover that there are amazing things to come in your life. Just be yourself...

Be Yourself Assignment

Write out five things that you like about yourself and remember to be really positive.

1.

2.

3.

4.

5.

Write out a little paragraph about who you think you are, be honest with yourself. Try to point out good things that others have told you in a yearbook maybe or it could even be just the things that your mom or grandmother told you when you thought they were just being nice. It's okay to feel good about yourself and these things are all true!!!!

You Are What You Think You Are! *

You really are! No matter who says what about us it is in our own minds that we decide what we are like. The more you tell yourself that you aren't good enough, the more you will begin to believe it. If you look in a mirror and tell yourself you are ugly, stupid, fat or anything else negative the more you will notice that this becomes true. You have the power to tell yourself who and what you are. Guaranteed. If you close your eyes and tell yourself that you are beautiful or handsome and really believe it, you will look at yourself completely differently. You will be beautiful or handsome when you see yourself. Try this today, and every day to come. Everything we think and feel is in our control. We always will control our own thoughts so this can be a powerful tool to remember. You may think that just saying something to yourself will not change how you look and it may not, but it will change what YOU see. You will no longer be focusing on all that you think is wrong, and don't forget that people will always see you for who you are. I have been so low sometimes that I honestly wondered why people wanted to be around me. They would be talking to me, telling me a story or something and I would be thinking "Geez do they not see how awful I look," or all the flaws that I saw. Soo not true. They were around me because they liked me for me and they thought I was great! Our self talk will eat us alive if it is all negative so please don't let these bad thoughts ruin your self image. Trust me it takes a very long time to get it back. Next time you look in the mirror take a deep breath, smile, and tell yourself how great you are. If you see someone looking down or feeling insecure then tell them too. You are what you think you are...

    This may seem like a lot to do but it is really easy, the more you tell yourself that you are great the more greatness you will see. When you catch yourself feeling low or not liking what you see in the mirror just change your thoughts. You are in control of these thoughts and your self image. When you have something big come up like a play, or a public event just remember to tell yourself how confident and capable you are. You are amazing at what you do. Once you really believe something about yourself others will see it to. How could they not?

    Have you noticed how some people look like they could take on the world and you wish you could be just like them? I wonder what kinds of thoughts they have going through their heads. Do you think they don't believe in themselves and think they aren't good enough? No way! They know who they are and what they want and they believe they are everything they can be. You can't be something that you are not but you can be everything that you want to be. Isn't that a good feeling. Watch and see how many people notice your new image now. They will start to look at you and wonder how they could be more like the way you are. It is important to remember that everything you feel and think about yourself will be exactly how you become. Good or bad, so why not only good. It's in you so you just need to bring it out. You're amazing!!!

"Whether you think you can or whether you think you can't

You are right!"

Henry Ford

"Believe in your dreams and they **MAY** come true...

Believe in yourself and they **WILL** come true"

Anonymous

*You Are What You Think You Are Assignment *

Now write out five things that you wish you could say about yourself but say it like you already are. These are called affirmations and they help us to become what we want to be. The more we tell ourselves what we are, the more we become like that. If you have a weakness you can make it better just by changing the way you think about it.

Example: I am a confident person who enjoys talking in front of people...

1.

2.

3.

4.

5.

Writing out what you want to be and affirming to yourself that it is true is the best thing you can do. You will become exactly what you want to be. You are what you think you are...

Affirmations

Have you ever heard of affirmations? They are declarations that something is true about ourselves. Which basically means it is a statement that we believe to be true about ourselves. We can use affirmations to reprogram our minds and our self images. This was another thing that I had to learn myself in order to get to where I am today. I used to be really hard on myself about everything that I was and everything I never thought I could do. I learned about affirmations in another course I took and have honestly been a changed person. It's unreal how something so small can change the way we feel and think about ourselves for the better. I will teach you what I have learned throughout this book so that you too can be a better person...

* Here are some examples of affirmations...

- I am a smart and capable person

- I can achieve all that I want to achieve

- I am very healthy

- I can write very well

- I am an important person in this world

- I can be patient in a difficult situation

- I am a good listener and friend

- I can handle anything that comes my way*

Saying anything in the present tense can shape and change you until what you are saying is true. If there is something you are lacking then just say it to yourself as if you weren't. Wait and see how quickly that weakness becomes a thing of the past. All you need to do is tell yourself what you want to be and it will be. Trust me... Try to do these affirmations on a regular basis, in order to change the way you think you have to do the work. You can write your own affirmations out on paper or cards and place them where you will see them everyday. Don't forget to pass your new found knowledge on to your loved ones, as I'm sure everyone can benefit from this.

Even simple things can be affirmed. You can say or write things like: I am a great friend, I am a great boyfriend/girlfriend, I am beautiful, I am so funny, I am very smart, I eat healthy foods, I am in good shape...and the list goes on and on. Remember that whether it is true at this moment does not matter because the more we affirm it as if it is already true the faster it will become true. You Can Do This!!

'You can be whatever you want to be'

* If You Can Think It You Can Achieve It! *

When I was about 21 I took a course called Thought Patterns For A Successful Career. It was a very intense class for where I was in my life, but I did get one thing out of it. If you can think it you can achieve it. It is so true. Kind of like this book that I am writing. I always dreamed of being a writer when I was young but never truly thought that I could do it. It was a fantasy to me because I thought only "other" people could accomplish great things. Here I am today and because I really thought I could do it, I can. If there is anything that you ever really want to do and you can see it then you really can do it. Don't ever let yourself, or anyone else tell you that it can't be done. Anything you want is possible if you can think it. That is the beauty of being human, we are so capable of anything it is not even funny. We are the rulers of our own destiny!!!

When you get to that point in your life that you know exactly what you want to do then just see it in your mind. Picture yourself actually doing it and before you know it your dream will come true. Even seeing yourself running the whole entire country is not too far fetched because if you can see yourself doing it then it can be done. How do you think all of our great leaders became who they are. I bet they knew deep down that they could do anything they wanted. No one is going to be able to stop you from doing great things, because you won't let them.

If you are still not believing in yourself now that is okay too. Changing the way we think is a hard thing to do and it doesn't happen over night. It took me a very long time to realize that I can be and do whatever I wish, and it will take you some time too. Just not as long as me I hope.

From now on you are in complete control of your life and what is to come. No matter how far away your future may be just remember that it will be waiting for you and one day everything you want for yourself will be there. Keep thinking positive thoughts and you will achieve all that you want to achieve. Maybe you can't think of exactly what it is you do want for yourself and that is okay. Don't worry because when you really decide there will be no one to hold you back. You will know that;

ANYTHING IS POSSIBLE!!

Think Positive!!!

There are so many books out there that many people have read and have learned a very important secret from. The power of Positive thinking. How could you ever go wrong if you always thought, or tried really hard to, think positive. I remember going to a car show when I was about eighteen and Zachary Ty Brian was there. He played Brad on Home Improvement the Television show. Anyways he gave me an autographed picture and on it he wrote "Think Poz!" At the time I thought it was kinda cheesy but now I wish I would have seen it for what it really meant. Life is so much better when you think positively. In any situation, even the most horrible ones you can find a positive thing to reflect on. Try to start your day off with a positive thought and notice how happier you start to feel. If you have a negative friend or family member or anyone else in your life right now try to explain to them that you don't like their negative energy around you. You can offer this advice to them too but if they continue to be negative just ignore them. The whole world will not change but you can for you. Eventually the bad energies will disappear. No one can take your positivity away from you because you are in control of you. That's awesome hey!? This is not going to be easy at first but if you try really hard you can do it. In addition the more positive energy you give out the more positive things that will come to you. We will get into that more as we go on and you will see what I mean. I'm sure you have heard the technical term "for every positive there is a negative," so just switch it up: "for every negative there is a positive." Try really hard, okay, because the more you can be positive the more energy you will have for living your life to the fullest.

*Let's Practice Turning Negative Thoughts and Comments into Positive Ones *

1. My life is so crappy right now I wish I could be someone else!

2. My job is so awful it is the worst job in the whole world.

3. I am not as smart as Becky, she always gets better marks than I do.

It may seem hard to turn these thoughts around but it is very easy. There will always be something positive about a situation. Maybe it is just that you will learn what it is you do not like. Comparing is a downward spiral and will only get worse as you grow up. Try to be as positive as you can possibly be and you will only go up from here! Even when you feel like your world is about to come crashing down you can pick yourself up and think about the good in your life. Be thankful for all that is good and the negatives will be ancient history...

Law of Attraction

Have you heard of this before? Everyone experiences it every day, they just might not understand it. When we say things like, "That was meant to be," or "It was Fate" that was the Law of Attraction working. Every minute of every day it is at work. Either in favor or against us, and that is up to us to make sure it is always in our favor. When we send out thoughts or words about what we want, then we shall receive. Only we can decide what kinds of things they will be. If you send out negative messages, then you will get negative things coming back. It works the same for positive messages. Those who figure this out and learn to use it will be able to control their own lives and what is going to happen in it. You will see amazing results from using the techniques associated with "Law of Attraction." So let's begin first by understanding exactly what it means.

The definition of "Law of Attraction" is:

"I attract attention to my life whatever I give my attention, energy and focus to, whether positive or negative."

This statement will take you far if you can really understand what it means. When we use our words, thoughts or feelings we are producing positive or negative vibes. We all know what vibes are and we all feel them. If you can understand that our vibes control what happens in our lives then you will understand the Law of Attraction. We need to start to send out only positive vibes so that only positive things come back our way. Isn't that such an easy concept for us to understand?! Exciting isn't it. To start off we need to learn to change our way of thinking and even our way of feeling. "The universe" can even feel our emotions. The universe is where our vibes travel to and from, believe it or not this is true. When we think positive or negatives thoughts, or use positive or negative words they are sent out into the universe. This is how the Law of Attraction works. If we are sending out all negative vibes we will only see more and more negatives in our lives. If we are sending out only positive vibes we will guaranteed only see positive things to come. This can work with anything at all. Use this new skill and watch in amazement how different your life can be. We cannot magically create something that was never meant to be so just keep that in mind if you think it is not working for you at all times. Let's try to see how we can change what we are sending out to our universe:

"I don't like failing all my courses..."

Chances are you will see more failure even though you are saying you don't like to fail. If we word it differently we can see a positive difference.

"I am so happy that I am passing all of my courses and doing my best…"

Using words like don't, and not will send out the message the wrong way, the universe still hears you, but only hears the part after don't. I don't want a mean boyfriend/girlfriend will be heard as, I want a mean boyfriend/girlfriend. See what I mean. Saying, I want a nice boyfriend/girlfriend will get you what you wish. Think of the universe as a Genie, like in the movie Aladdin. It is there to grant you your wishes. If your genie asked you your first wish and you said, "I don't want to be poor anymore" then you wasted your first wish. If you rephrased your wish, "I want five hundred dollars" Your wish would come true. Right? How easy is that!? Be specific in what you do want and never mind what you don't want, and you shall receive.

So get the Law of Attraction working for you. It is always working, just start making it work to your advantage by using your 'good vibes.'

Let's try another one okay:

"I have no money and I never will."

* Our new way of using the Law of Attraction:

"Money comes easily and frequently and I have more than enough."

You may think that there is no way that just by saying that you have money, you will get some. But you will! I promise. I did not believe this at all when I first learned about it but once I really tried to do it, things came my way. Not just money, but good relationships, things I needed, my kids being really good, less bills, etc. Without doing anything more than sending out positive energy and thoughts. Your words are most important because they are said out loud. Catch yourself when you use words like, I don't have, or I won't get, or why can't I do…the list goes on. Change your words and you will change your life. Start saying, writing, and thinking about all the things you Can have and Will have, and Are going to do. This is so easy to do it seems silly but we haven't been taught this throughout our lives. It will help you like it has helped me if you use it. Even when you slip a little, don't worry because you can get right back into it again. I still catch myself sometimes sending out negative vibes and I usually say "I take it back!" as soon as I realize it. That's my way of cancelling it out.

Do you think you can do this? Do you want to see a difference in your life no matter who you are, or where you live, or where you came from? Great things will and are going to happen for you, you'll see…

See if you can turn these negative statements into positive ones. Remember that our universe hears us always no matter what.

Negative   **Positive**
I never win anything!

I don't ever pass any of my tests

I don't like being picked on by other kids

There will be no stopping you now. You have your own personal genie waiting to grant you all of your wishes.

Gratitude

This is HUGE! It is one of the best secrets to life that you will ever learn. It is the most important thing that I want you to get out of this book. All that we have in this world we should be grateful for. The more we are truly and deeply grateful for, the more we will receive. I don't just mean material things and possessions, I mean anything that you can think of. The first time I heard about gratitude was while reading a book called 'Simple Abundance' I was going through a really bad break up with my little boy's dad and I was completely lost. I didn't know whether I was coming or going. I had my daughter who was five years old and my son who was a year and a half. I felt so alone and hopeless it was horrible. So I bought this book at a second hand store for fifty cents and decided to read it to take my mind off of it all. Well it is worth a zillion dollars to me now that's for sure. The main concept of this book was Gratitude. Almost the whole book.

It was amazing how much it made me think. The author said to go and get a notebook and every night before bed write five things you were grateful for that day. It was called the gratitude journal. It's so awesome how much there is to be grateful for that we usually take for granted. I was really stressed out in life at the time but I managed to actually find five things. My kids, my health and the fact that I could be free from such a jerk and I was grateful just to be in a safe place. As time went on I found even more things to be grateful for. Some days it was a different entry then others like, "I am grateful for not totally losing it on the kids today!!" Or I am grateful for my precious kitty, or just about the same old thing if I was having a bad day. The cool part was that the more I wrote about my gratitude the more good things that were coming my way. It was so exciting.

What are you grateful for? I bet there are a thousand things in your life you are thankful to have, people, possessions, qualities, traits, anything you can think of. Why don't you try to think of six things that you are grateful for right now.

1.

2.

3.

4.

5.

6.

It will make a huge difference in your life when you see clearly about all the good things that you already have. When we are grateful for all that is ours we will have more than we could wish for. Trying to just 'fake' gratitude will not work, you need to be truly and deeply grateful...

Starting your own gratitude journal is one of the best things that you can do for yourself. I still have one and I probably always will. It's important to see what we already have around us, and to remember how lucky we are. You will only receive more good things when you are already grateful for the ones you already have...

No Doubt!

Most of us know this term used either for a band featuring Gwen Stefani or a phrase to say That's Right! But in this book it is to describe a very important life lesson. Never doubt yourself. Ever. Once you believe that you can do something don't give up. The minute you doubt yourself you will notice these wishes and dreams do not come true. I know it is hard at first and I will be the first one to admit that. I always doubted that I could do something amazing because I thought only other important people could achieve great things. Doubt will eat our dreams alive, and our self esteem as well. If you never doubt yourself or the things that you can do then you can never be disappointed. You can do absolutely anything you set out to do. I promise you that, but when doubt creeps in it can take over. Don't let it, Okay? You deserve all that you want, and wish to do, why let such a little word bring you down. I still catch myself doubting every once in a while and it is not a good feeling at all. Then, I just stop myself from thinking I can't do something, or whatever negative thought I am having and pick up where I left off. No Doubt!! If you doubt yourself, you are allowing the universe and everyone in it to doubt you as well. Sometimes I use others doubt to my advantage. If they show any doubt for what I say I am going to do then I use that as motivation to get it done faster. I will never doubt myself again and I don't want you to either. You can do this!*

*** When in doubt, Think positive ***

What's Meant to Be Will Be... *

This is so important it's not even funny!! Would you really want something in your life that wasn't totally good for you? I don't think so... If you really want that girlfriend or boyfriend and you've done everything to try and make it happen, and it doesn't, do you feel unworthy and confused as to what is wrong with you? I know I have so many times. I used to cry and cry and try to figure out what I could've done differently or decided to dye my hair or lose ten more pounds, get a new wardrobe or whatever it took to get them to like me. But it still didn't happen. After many of these horrible situations and with less and less self esteem, I had an acquaintance tell me four precious words (yes I was crying on the shoulder of an almost perfect stranger) WASN'T MEANT TO BE!!! How cool is that?! Of course I was crying and insisting that YES it was, but the more I kept this statement in the back of my mind the easier it was to spring back after a loss. What a weight off my shoulders when I realized it had nothing to do with me, or the way I looked, dressed, talked, walked. It just wasn't meant to be. The beauty of this is that it allows us to be fully open to something when it truly is meant to be. This goes for everything, and trust me there is a lot more to come. Didn't get that job you wanted and you're completely bummed... that's okay because it wasn't meant to be. Almost instantly the right one will come along. Didn't get the car or puppy you really wanted?? Chances are there was something terribly wrong with it, and if you can accept this fully an even better one will come along. If we don't let go when something doesn't turn out how we wish then we are really blocking things that are trying to come to us. So say your good byes to the things you thought you couldn't live without and say Hello to the great things that were always...Meant To Be...

Treat Others as You Would Like to Be Treated

Did your parents or grandparents ever tell you this when you were little? They should have if they didn't. It is so important to use this motto from this day forward and teach others about it as well. If you treat people good, then good things will happen to you forever. Maybe people will not be nice or polite to you back but that is alright, it just means that they don't know this secret. When you are kind to others, you will feel good about yourself, and when you feel good about yourself you give off good vibes. Remember what we learned about good vibes? Some people are not very nice and some are actually evil, especially in this day and age. They will never understand this saying, either because they were not taught it or they just plain don't care. Even when you encounter these people in your life don't forget this phrase. Treat others how you would like to be treated. If there is a grumpy old man at a corner store and he is always rude to everyone, it does not give you the right to be rude back. It is his problem that he is so miserable and only he can change how he is. You can still be polite and kind to him and everyone else that wants to be like him. They are sending out negative vibes and you will know that they will never receive anything they truly want, but you will. If there is someone who looks upset, lost, or confused, then ask them if they are alright. Even a perfect stranger. This doesn't mean you get in their car or go to their home, because that will always be dangerous, but asking someone if they are alright is kind and it may make their whole day better. Most of all treat your family, friends, and the people closet to you as you wish to be treated. How could you ever go wrong? Remember that if someone shows you no kindness or concern, that is okay because you can 'Kill them with Kindness'. I have met so many ignorant, miserable people in my twenty nine years, and I often wondered what I ever did to deserve the way they were treating me. I realize now that I had nothing to do with the way they were. It was not my job to fix them and all I could do was resist the urge to tell them off, and just be nice. Now I see why my mom taught me this important lesson as I grew up. I am everything I want to be, and I receive all that I wish for. I know it's hard but just try. When you are in the mall, at a library, at school, at work, or anywhere else, treat people with kindness and respect. It's the only way to be....

****

Elders deserve our respect, and kindness at all times. Please don't ever forget this. They have lived long lives and are very wise people, and one day we too will be old and fragile. Hold doors open for them, help them if they need help, ask them how they are doing, or even just a smile. The world can only get better if we are all a little more kind to each other. Stand up for anyone that is not treated nicely, and always lend a helping hand. You will see how good your life will be when you treat others how you would like to be treated....

Never Talk Badly About Others
EVER

Seriously don't talk about other people, or gossip, or criticize them, or anything else along these lines. Besides the fact that it is not nice, it also creates very bad karma. Do you know what karma is? It will come back to get you every time whether you believe it or not! A native elder once told me something that completely changed the way I think about things. From that day on I refrained from talking badly about anyone. Including myself. I was in a bad situation at the time and basically didn't know if I was coming or going. This lady and I happened to be in the same place at the same time, and now I believe I was in that mess just so I could meet her and learn this lesson. I didn't start a conversation with her but she came and sat down beside me and said I looked like I needed her help. I was kind of stubborn at that time in my life and didn't think I needed anyone's help. She told me a "little secret." She said that when people talk about other people they are almost wishing bad things upon themselves. At first I didn't see how that was possible, but I realized she knew exactly what she was talking about. She gave me a lot of examples to support her secret. If someone sees a young girl walking down the street with three little children, and they say, "Oh look at that girl she is so stupid for having those kids. She must get around, or not have been brought up right!" Then they are setting themselves up for bad things. This lady said that you can guarantee the person who judged will one day be walking down the street with babies, all alone too. When you see someone with bad skin, or bad hair and you laugh about it at their expense, know for sure that one day you too will have bad skin and bad hair as well. You will be put in that person's shoes so that you will know how it feels. Think of something in your life that has bothered you. Did you ever tease or make fun of someone with the same problem? If you did then you know why you are faced with the same bad thing. If you haven't had this happen to you then keep up the good work, because you obviously don't judge or talk bad about others, and you already know the secret. I believe this is true because I used to talk about people when I was young. Maybe we all do but I learned real fast that it can only set me up for disaster in my own life. My older sister was quite the wild child, and I was always the "good" one. I used to play on that and make her realize that she wasn't as good. Now that I look back I see that all the things I would bug her about; bad grades, always in trouble, were starting to happen to me later on. Back then I just thought the whole world was against me and I didn't deserve to be treated like her, but I see now that I did deserve it. I said cruel things to her and they all happened to me at some point in my life. When she had her first child at twenty one without the father around I looked down on her. Told her she wasn't very smart and would struggle forever, and that she made a bad choice. Before I knew it, I was pregnant, and the father turned out to be no good for us either. I was twenty one...

I have learned my lesson, and luckily I learned it soon in life. Do not talk badly about others, or look down on them for their choices. Whether they are bad choices or not it is not your place in this world to judge. Just be grateful of the good things and wish good things for others. You can't take all your words back, so just don't say them at all. You will never understand the way things feel unless you are experiencing them for yourself. It is not fair to pretend like you know why people are in the boats that they are, because you really don't know. Unless you want everything you talk about, or laugh about, to happen to you then I suggest you say nothing about others. Only good things, and then good things will come to you. Just like our grandmothers probably said to us all. "If you don't have anything nice to say, then don't say anything at all!"

Remember this statement forever, and ever. You will be the nicest, best person that you can be and you will enjoy true happiness. I am glad that I got to teach others these lessons and secrets that I have learned. If you follow them you will be as happy and content as I am today. Don't forget to tell yourself how special you are, and love who you were born to be. I wish nothing but great things for you, and I know you will be a shining star in your world someday soon. *

I have included some pages for you to use as your gratitude journal. Try to do this every night before bed, or at least whenever you can. Name five things you are grateful for during that day and watch and see how many more you will be grateful for the next. You now know as I do the great secrets of life and you can only go up from here. You can be all that you wish to be because you are a great person, and you deserve great things always. And just remember:

The sky is the limit....

Yesterday Is History

Yesterday is history, Tomorrow is a mystery, Today is a gift...Enjoy. I remember getting a gift one year and this was written on it. I am not sure where this quote came from, but once again it is so true. If you truly know that you cannot change your past, and that you cannot predict your future, it really helps you to just live in the moment. That doesn't mean that you will not have goals and just roam around, but we all have to remember that life has no guarantees. This maybe your last day and mine, on earth, so we need to try to live each day to the fullest. What a waste of some days I've had. Just sitting around sad or feeling low, or bothered by something that had happened years earlier or how I was going to achieve my goals by such and such a year. There is really no point in wondering how or why you are going to do something by a specific time and put extra pressure on yourself if it is not done by then. Just live your life and it will unfold as planned....Putting too much pressure on yourself is just cruel. You know what you want and how you're going to get it so just give yourself the time for it to happen. It can be hazardous to our health to not give ourselves a break once in a while. As long as you are on the right path everything will work out. We need to give ourselves credit and pay attention to how far we've come. Wasn't too long ago that we were finger painting or running in the playground carefree and happy, so it won't be too long until our dreams have come true. Enjoy the journey you are on and then you will be able to enjoy yourself when you get to where you are headed. Every one of us has something from out past that we wish we could erase. It's never gonna happen though!! When we are aware of that we can just focus on how much stronger we have become because of it. There is no such thing as a time machine (even though that would be the coolest thing ever!). But we can never go back and change things, nor can we rush into the future with that same time machine to see where we have gotten to. Just take the good out of the past and leave the rest behind where it belongs. Our futures await us all and anything really is possible so don't try too hard to rush things along. Enjoy every day like it was your last and you will not have any regrets when you do get to your future someday….

My Gratitude Journal

My Gratitude Journal

My Gratitude Journal

My Gratitude Journal

My Gratitude Journal

My Gratitude Journal

My Gratitude Journal

My Gratitude Journal

Bibliography and Other Related References

Law of Attraction:
   Michael J. Losier

Simple Abundance; A Daybook of Comfort and Joy:
   Sarah Ban Breathnach

'Thought Patterns for a successful Career'
The Pacific Institute
   Lou Tice

The Secret

Printed in the United States
132737LV00007B/290/P

9 781424 188444